CREATIVE
JAPANESE FLOWER ARRANGEMENT

Creative
Japanese Flower Arrangement

by

NORMAN SPARNON

SHUFUNOTOMO CO., LTD.
Tokyo, Japan

Also by Norman Sparnon
Japanese Flower Arrangement, Classical and Modern
The Beauty of Wildflowers
The Magic of Camellias (with E. G. Waterhouse)
The Poetry of Leaves
Ikebana with Roses (with Kasumi Teshigahara)
A Guide to Japanese Flower Arrangement
   Translated from the Japanese:
The Soul of Rikka by Fujiwara, Yuchiku

Third printing, 1984

Published by Shufunotomo Co., Ltd.
1-chome, Surugadai, Kanda, Chiyoda-ku, Tokyo, Japan

Printed in Japan

TO
SOFU TESHIGAHARA
FOUNDER
SOGETSU SCHOOL
1900–1979

CONTENTS

Foreword by Hiroshi Teshigahara : *7*
Author's Foreword : *9*
Introduction : *11*

PART ONE : CREATIVE ARRANGEMENTS

1. Sculptured Root, Acacia, Eucalyptus and Banksias : *19*
2. Weeping Mulberry, Acacia, Eucalyptus and Poinsettias : *21*
3. Camellias and Dried Sunflowers : *23*
4. Fasciated Hoop Pine, Cornflowers and Leucadendron : *25*
5. Dodder Vine and Poinsettias : *27*
6. Dodder Vine and Arum Lilies : *29*
7. Strelitzia and Lotus Pods : *31*
8. Albizzia Pods and Lasciandra : *33*
9. Wisteria Vine and Hydrangea : *35*
10. Pussy Willow, Pansies and Violets : *37*
11. Water Lilies and Sculpture : *39*
12. Dried Sunflowers and Dahlia : *41*
13. Gypsophila and Chrysanthemums : *43*
14. Scrap Metal, Daffodils and Dried Sunflowers : *45*
15. Poinciana Pods and Sunflowers : *47*
16. Pomegranates and Scrap Metal : *49*
17. Edgeworthia and Strelitzia : *51*
18. Scrap Metal and Sunflower : *53*
19. Camellia : *55*
20. Dried Aspidistra Leaves and Poppies (1) : *57*
21. Dried Aspidistra Leaves and Poppies (2) : *59*
22. Roses, Asparagus Fern and Edgeworthia : *61*
23. Scrap Metal and Cornflowers : *63*
24. Palm Spathes and Acacia : *65*
25. Scrap Metal and Sunflower : *67*
26. Stirrups, Bit and Woody Pear : *69*
27. Camellias : *71*

28. Japonica and Camellias : *73*
29. Dried Aspidistra Leaves, Acacia and Dutch Iris : *75*
30. Nandina and Iris : *77*
31. Sunflowers : *79*
32. Fox-face, Dried Monstera and Strelitzia : *81*
33. Albizzia Pods, Verticordia and Monstera : *83*
34. Eucalyptus Bark and Strelitzia : *85*
35. Root and Hoop Pine : *87*
36. Aspidistra Leaves, Daisies and Cornflowers : *89*
37. Monstera Leaf and Agiratum : *91*
38. Carnations and Metal Strapping : *93*
39. Iris Orientalis : *95*
40. Pussy Willow and Camellia : *97*

PART TWO : BASIC LESSONS

Basic Lessons : *101*
Lesson 1. Moribana. Basic Upright Style : *103*
Lesson 2. Moribana. Basic Slanting Style : *105*
Lesson 3. Moribana. Upright Style, First Variation : *107*
Lesson 4. Moribana. Upright Style, Second Variation : *109*
Lesson 5. Moribana. Upright Style, Third Variation : *111*
Lesson 6. Moribana. Upright Style, Fourth Variation : *113*
Lesson 7. Moribana. Upright Style, Fifth Variation : *115*
Lesson 8. Moribana. Upright Style, Sixth Variation : *117*
Lesson 9. Moribana. Slanting Style, Sixth Variation : *119*
Lesson 10. Moribana. Horizontal Style, Sixth Variation : *121*
Lesson 11. Floating Arrangement : *123*
Lesson 12. Morimono : *125*
Lesson 13. Moribana. Eighth Variation, Two-Container Arrangement : *127*
Lesson 14. Nageire. Basic Upright Style : *129*
Lesson 15. Nageire. Basic Slanting Style : *131*

Index : *133*

FOREWORD

About Norman Sparnon

I am personally extremely happy to see this book published. As we all know, Norman Sparnon's place in the field of Ikebana is an important one, resulting in a richly deserved international reputation.

I myself knew of him early because my father, Sōfū, often spoke of him to us, praising the power and the humanity of his work. One of the reasons for this strength is that he has studied so deeply, so seriously—not only within the various forms of Ikebana but, more importantly, within the history of Ikebana itself. To this appreciation he has added a very long familiarity with Japan.

How Mr. Sparnon came to Japan and in what manner he arrived at this profound understanding of Ikebana, I do not properly know, but looking at the work itself I see that any hankering for the exoticism of Asian flower arrangement played little part. Rather, there is a truly creative feeling for flowers and plants themselves, a matter of feeling for them and of learning to feel with them. Herein lies the originality of his work, and the rightness of his international reputation.

Postwar Japan has already lost many of its traditional virtues—a bad thing, but out of bad things often comes good. That Ikebana tradition continues in the work of Mr. Sparnon is one of these, one which makes me personally very happy.

Hiroshi Teshigahara
Headmaster
Sōgetsu School

AUTHOR'S FOREWORD

My first real encounter with Ikebana was at the first major post-war exhibition of the Sōgetsu School in the Mitsukoshi Department Store on the Ginza in 1949.

My wife and I had been studying Ikebana for only a short period of time and the exhibition proved to be a highly stimulating artistic experience. Different in concept from any other style of floral art I had previously seen the exhibition impressed me in several diverse ways—the creative thinking individually expressed in the arrangements, the visual impact of the presentation of the exhibition and the feeling expressed in the arrangement of the flowers.

Three works by the founder and headmaster of the School, Sofu Teshigahara, dominated the exhibition. One, an arrangement of camellias in a stone vase designed by Mr. Sofu was particularly beautiful. Another large work titled "Abyss" was very impressive and the third, an extremely modern work of scrap metal, wheels and pampas titled "Locomotive" was highly creative. This dramatic move away from the traditional Ikebana styles placed the Sōgetsu School in the vanguard of the modern movement which revolutionized the whole world of Ikebana. Under the guidance of its headmaster Ikebana became a formative art providing a stimulating challenge.

Through the encouragement and guidance of the headmaster Mr. Sofu my own involvement became complete and my life was to change and be enriched by the experience. Now the great master and his beautiful daughter Miss Kasumi have gone but the school continues to flourish under the guidance of his talented son, Hiroshi Teshigahara.

Throughout the book I have quoted from the teachings of Mr. Sofu as explained in his beautiful book "Sofu, His Boundless World of Flowers and Form" published by Kodansha in 1966 and from the teaching of the new Headmaster Mr. Hiroshi Teshigahara. The remainder of the quotations are my random thoughts gleaned from experience in teaching and study over the past thirty years.

This, then, is but a modest effort to present the teachings of a great Master by a grateful student in the hope that it may encourage and help Western students to carry on with the study of this beautiful art.

I am extremely grateful to my wife, Mary, who is my best and at times worst critic, for her helpful suggestions and for bearing the brunt of my frustrations while I was arranging and particularly photographing the contents of this book.

To our dear friend, Isla Stuart, my gratitude for her able assistance, willingly given, in the editing.

Sydney 1982   Norman Sparnon

INTRODUCTION

A true understanding of Ikebana is firmly based upon a deep awareness of nature. It is this awareness that endows the disciples of Ikebana with an inexhaustible source of inspiration. Inspiration by itself, however, is not enough. For the artist inspiration must be given an external expression, must be communicated. This is both the joy and the duty of the artist and in the final analysis the artist's worth is measured both by the quality of his inspiration and by his ability to master the techniques for communicating this inspiration. The Ikebana arranger is not content just to see a beautiful flower growing. Instead, he wants to communicate the beauty and the meaning of the flower to others. It is the arranger's sensitivity to beauty, combined with an emotional urge toward creativeness that can refine a natural design to the point where it transcends nature. This philosophy is embodied in the understanding of the Japanese word *Shusshō*, a word borrowed from the vocabulary of the Buddhist religion and widely used in the Ikebana vocabulary. Literally meaning "the emergence of life" it connotes that all plants are considered to have life similar to human life. Effort must be made to read the minds of the plants; to go beyond their superficial botanical aspects and so to grasp the meaning of their being, spiritually as well as materially.

Are there principles of flower arrangement which make such communication possible? The answer is very much in the affirmative. Every school of Japanese flower arrangement, whether classical or modern, has successfully applied such principles. All arrangements in this book are based upon the principles of the Sōgetsu School.

There are two basic approaches to Ikebana. The objective approach which we shall call "naturalistic" takes nature as its model and, though it may idealize nature's patterns, never violates the laws of natural growth. The subjective approach, variously called "expressionistic" or "free style", utilizes the forms of nature to create patterns freely to express the designer's subjective sense of design, unrestricted by the laws of natural growth. The Sōgetsu School has always placed great emphasis upon this twofold aspect of Ikebana and upon the student's having a thorough understanding of the principles involved in both approaches. In the naturalistic approach, emphasis is placed upon the way plants actually grow in nature. It is the primary function of a naturalistic arrangement to express this feeling of natural growth. In the expressionistic approach one's sense of fitness and good design is the only limiting factor in arriving at the finished arrangement. Between these two approaches there are of course many gradations, all equally valid depending upon the given situation. Outside of these approaches, there is only the chaos of fads and momentary novelties. These must be avoided and never confused with serious Ikebana.

A branch placed in a vase in such a way as to express the feeling of the way it actually grows in its natural habitat may indeed be very beautiful. When expertly arranged it can move the viewer both spiritually and emotionally. Or the same branch may be inverted and placed in or against a vase in a manner that is diametrically opposed to its natural way of growing and the results may prove stimulating both in design and in dramatic effect.

Whether the approach be naturalistic or expressionistic the aesthetic value of the completed arrangement is determined by the arranger's sensitivity to beauty and principles of good design.

The function of good Ikebana is the creation of beauty and good Ikebana is good design. The creative artist imposes upon nature a pattern of his own dimension. Creative work is not achieved only by reading textbooks and following instructions. It must also be an expression of emotional impulse. But sound principles can be the springboard for true creativity.

How then do we go about achieving an infinite variety of patterns based upon a few principles? The following paragraphs are an attempt to analyze this question briefly in a way that will be helpful to all serious students of Ikebana, particularly to students of the Sōgetsu and other modern schools. All the arrangements shown in the body of this book will be, both in their purpose and design, a practical demonstration of this analysis.

The most basic philosophy of Ikebana is embodied in two Japanese words: *seishin*, meaning "spirit" and *chōwa*, "harmony". But the deeper meanings and overtones of the words are more important than their literal translations. In Ikebana, *seishin* is an understanding of the spiritual soul of a flower also expressed in *shusshō*, and *chōwa* is the harmony between man and nature. The inner meaning of these two Oriental concepts becomes apparent only through incessant study.

The most basic principle of good Ikebana is balance. Let us begin here.

BALANCE There are three types of balance: symmetrical, asymmetrical, and radial. All three are used at one time or another in most schools of Ikebana but it is the asymmetrical that is the underlying form of all schools.

In nature symmetry may be readily seen in almost any flower or leaf and in many trees. Balance is symmetrical when half of an object is an exact replica of the other half, usually in mirror image.

Asymmetry exists when the object is balanced without the two halves being identical. This type of balance, so prevalent in Ikebana, is also known as active or dynamic balance. It invites a more vigorous reaction than symmetrical balance, which is formal, passive, static. Asymmetry infers movement and, at times, a spontaneous casualness. These are two important aspects of good Ikebana.

The third type of balance is comparatively rare in Ikebana. Balance is said to be radial when all parts radiate from a central point, a good example being the petals of a daisy. Such balance possesses a definite target or focal point.

Balance is produced by an interaction of parts and in Ikebana these parts are principal branches of varying lengths, usually three in number, sometimes with one or more supplementary branches.

The placement of the principal branches, generally with a strong forward movement, usually produces the asymmetrical pattern that is the most common type of balance found in all schools of Ikebana. Hence it is that the only important difference between the various schools lies in the angles of placement and method of expression.

VARIETY AND UNITY Another of the basic considerations of good Ikebana is the combination of unity and variety. As explained previously, *chōwa* is a concept of Oriental philosophy requiring harmony between man and nature. In Ikebana, as in other forms of Japanese art, this concept is often expressed in the phrase *Ten-Chi-Jin* (Heaven-Earth-Man), which describes the ideal state of the universe as one harmonious whole and is the condition of artistic unity toward which the flower arranger always strives. This philosophy is embodied in *Shumisen* the mythical Mount Mehru of the Buddhist and Hindu cosmology on which the classical *Rikka* the original Ikebana is based.

Variety and unity may be achieved in several ways:

1) By exercising restraint in the number of materials used in an arrangement. With the exception of the *Rikka* style, Japanese flower arrangements traditionally contain one, two or at the most three, materials. Even the modern styles seldom use more than three. Too much variety leads to chaos not unity.

2) By maintaining balance in the design.

3) By choosing materials that are in harmony with the basic idea of the arrangement.

4) By correct presentation, both in the selection of the container and in the choice of setting or background for the completed arrangement in order to focus attention on the basic idea. Remember that the container is not simply a receptacle for water. It is an integral part of the whole design and also serves to segregate the arrangement from its surroundings. And yet despite this segregation, the surroundings too play a vital part. The Japanese have always paid considerable attention to this problem of setting. For centuries the *tokonoma*, or recessed alcove, has provided the Japanese home with an ideal setting for Ikebana. On the exhibition bench elaborate steps are taken to insure that the arrangements are given the right setting.

Variety expresses strength by way of contrast. Unity expresses oneness, with the divergent elements taking their appointed places in the whole. The marriage of the two gives variety in unity, one of the ideal concepts in any work of art.

As a matter of fact, all the principles of Ikebana are synonymous with those of other Japanese art forms.

We have so far considered the principles of balance and variety in unity. The remaining principles in this analysis are the five plastic elements with which every artist works irrespective of his medium. We shall consider them here primarily in relation to Ikebana.

FORM   Form is basic structure before any embellishments are added. The principal branches—*Shin* (primary), *Soe* (secondary) and *Hikae* (tertiary) determine the form of an arrangement. In the words of Sofu Teshigahara, these three branches are the skeleton while the supplementary branches are the flesh. It is the method of construction, of combining these three branches into a single design, that creates the form. The principles governing the method of construction are variously determined by the different schools of Ikebana. The masters of these schools who devise the different principles are, in effect, the architects while the teachers and students are the builders.

It is precisely here that pseudo-Ikebana fails. The view that Ikebana is governed simply by a universal rule of three branches of varying lengths—usually defined as Heaven, Man and Earth—is tantamount to believing that merely roof, walls and floor will produce a beautiful building. The master mind of a great architect is required to devise the precise methods of construction. Master builders with consummate skills to execute the architect's plans are also essential. Similarly, in flower arranging it is only the following of basic principles and plans evolved by the great masters that can produce a true Ikebana for those principles determine an arrangement's form, produce its dominant characteristics and finally define it as Ikebana. In advanced Ikebana study, however, there comes the day when the architect no longer supplies precise blueprints to be followed exactly but instead merely roughs out the ideas and the methods of construction, leaving the actual builder with considerable creative freedom to interpret and execute the plan.

If form is structure, one will appreciate that the form of the component parts will influence the completed form. Hence the importance of giving considerable care to the selection of materials that have inherent good form. In naturalistic arrangements the branches or flowers should express the natural growth of the plant.

LINE AND MASS   Ikebana has generally been considered to be a linear style of flower arrangement and it is true that the linear style of Ikebana has wide appeal. Probably more than any other element, line has always been closely associated with Ikebana and most classical arrangements are purely linear in form. But in modern arrangements more scope is given to other principles of design in particular to mass. And yet, in a certain sense, mass is but a product of line. Line by confining space can express mass.

Branches strong in line and properly manipulated can give a feeling of vigorous or passive movement. Horizontal lines express tranquility and calmness; vertical lines, vigor and strength. But in the final analysis it is the oblique line that does most to create the dynamics of movement in an arrangement. Usually, then, this oblique line is the dominant element of any Ikebana design, one that generally requires an opposing or balancing diagonal to give the arrangement stability. This principle of design can be readily observed in all basic Ikebana patterns. It is an expression of movement, inherent in Ikebana since its inception, that is also found in mass arrangements.

The Japanese have always been endowed with a good sense of design strongly characterized by line. One of the reasons may be their early training in calligraphy. The study of their intricate ideographs is in itself a study in linear design as well as in the subtle balancing of masses.

Both line and mass are important plastic elements at the disposal of an artist and they play an equally important role in Ikebana design.

SPACE Space ranks with form as one of the two most important plastic elements. We live in a space-conscious era, not only of space beyond the earth but of space in our daily lives. In the buildings we enter, the houses we live in, the cities we inhabit we are constantly aware of spatial organization. Space is as important as the forms, colors, and textures that have been used to confine it.

In Ikebana, space is created by the placement of the three principal branches or through the elimination of non-essentials by cutting or trimming. By such elimination we utilize the space left by the object that has been removed. Space emphasizes form and form is structure. The basic principles of all schools of Ikebana guide the student in the placement of branches to construct a system of balance in which space is utilized to accent the basic idea.

COLOR This is not the place for a dissertation on color or color harmonies, which have been exhaustively discussed by many qualified authors. We are concerned here solely with the use of color as a basic element in Ikebana. Colors in nature are infinite. Their use in Ikebana is governed by the philosophical concept of *chōwa*, or harmony, which we have already mentioned. Harmony between man and nature is indeed profoundly affected by color. Since it has such a strong effect upon the beholder's own dispositions and emotions, color must be used with considerable thought.

As already indicated, it is important to begin with a basic plan or idea and to decide what mood one wishes to create. Is the effect to be stimulating or peaceful, loud or quiet, gay or dull, cool or warm, dramatic or unobtrusive? Related or harmonious colors tend to express a quiet, restful effect when strong intensities are avoided. Contrasting colors such as yellow and violet or yellow, blue and red are more dramatic and stimulating.

In classical Ikebana, colors are generally subdued, the arrangements tending to impart a feeling of tranquility and repose. Modern Ikebana is usually more dramatic in approach, using contrasting and warm colors. For this reason more color is used in present-day Ikebana than during any other phase of the art's long history. In classical Ikebana, as well as in other arts influenced by Buddhism, a color was seldom chosen fortuitously. All colors and designs were strictly regulated by detailed rules. This control still exists in the strictly classical styles of Ikebana. Five of the seven most famous arrangements in the old classical form of Rikka—the evergreen pine, symbol of longevity; the lotus, emblem of Buddhism; the cherry blossom; the iris and the narcissus—are basically without color contrast, relying purely on form and one-color harmony for their effects. The two exceptions are arrangements of autumn maple leaves in which all the colors of the season are used and of chrysanthemums in which many different colors are combined in a single arrangement, one popular combination being white, yellow, red, bronze, pink and lavender.

With the spread of Ikebana to the West it was probably the Japanese use of color more than any of the other design elements that attracted most attention. Popular Oriental color combinations that seemed to violate all Occidental theories of color harmony—such as red and yellow, orange and pink—have now become widely accepted, not only in flower arrangements but also in such popular Oriental textiles as the beautiful Thai silks. In the same way the West has gradually become used to color combinations that at first glance seemed to clash discordantly—say electric blue and bright orange. Such combinations, probably derived from the colors used in Buddhist iconography, are popular with the modern branches of classical Ikebana schools.

TEXTURE   Textural contrasts between different materials or between materials and container also play an important role in Ikebana. Working as closely as he does with the infinitely variable materials of nature, the Ikebana arranger deals with a broad range of textural qualities. Similarly, the gardens of Japan, surely among the most beautiful in the world, provide superb studies of spatial organization and textural contrasts.

In Ikebana only by holding a material in our hands can we fully appreciate its tactile values and qualities. By our sense of touch we come to know the strength of the pine, the delicacy of the camellia or rose, the smoothness of flax, the silkiness of willow or bamboo. In this way we find our true stimulus for selecting the most suitable background for an arrangement, for choosing subsidiary materials and for deciding upon a container, whether it be porcelain, terra cotta, bronze or bamboo. And it is also by our sense of touch that we decide whether the texture of one material accords with the form and color of another; whether there is a harmony of relationships in all the parts.

For example, for a simple wall arrangement using either a basket or a ceramic container, a rose or camellia might be quite suitable whereas the texture of pine cones might well not be so pleasing. Conversely, if the plan were for a mural against a textured wall, pine cones might be most appropriate. Their texture would be in character with the basic idea and the texture of the component parts would harmonize with each other. As a general rule, when more than one material is used in an arrangement the most effective results are obtained when the textures are related to each other. But it is also true that contrasting textures, such as dried sunflowers and camellias, may also be used effectively for variety and accent.

The foregoing is but a brief survey of a very intricate subject. As in all things, one learns best by doing and I hope that my comments will give readers a sense of participation in the creation of these arrangements and serve as a guide to their own creative Ikebana.

PART ONE : CREATIVE ARRANGEMENTS

Ikebana is at times representation and at times inter-pretation. Creative Ikebana should be interpretation. Those who do not strive to expand their experience remain limited by their environment. Ikebana is an awareness of nature and its practice requires emotional involvement. It is the inner feeling plus a deep understanding of the elements represented combined with skillful technique that makes Ikebana a rewarding experience.

Sculptured root, acacia, eucalyptus and banksias.

The Sōgetsu School in its promotion of Ikebana as a creative art divides its study into three phases: naturalistic styles which utilize only floral materials whether branches or flowers arranged in a naturalistic manner; floral material combined with non-floral objects and thirdly, objects of the arranger's own design used without floral materials. In this arrangement a free standing sculptured root covered with aluminium shim is combined with eucalyptus foliage, acacia and two scarlet banksias.

Ikebana is an art to be felt inwardly. It is not to be understood logically. An understanding of the basic principles while providing an involvement with nature is far removed from the mastery of the art. Fulfillment is reached through study, practice and experience.

Weeping mulberry, acacia, eucalyptus and poinsettias.

Mass, line and color, important ingredients of the study of Ikebana are expressed in this combination of bleached weeping mulberry, eucalyptus foliage, acacia and poinsettias. The spherical design emanated from the two hemispheres made of strips of metal welded in a basket-like weave. The colorful materials held together by a white lacquer vase provide a festive mood.

In every Ikebana arrangement there is line, color and an intangible spirit. It is the varying degree in which these are present that determines the quality of the work. One of the reasons that I find camellias so pleasing in Ikebana is that they have these things in just the right proportion. The best way of bringing out these three elements in any arrangement is to combine two different kinds of flowers.

Sofu

Camellias and dried sunflowers.

Dissimilar in form and texture, camellias and dried sunflowers provide an interesting and challenging combination. Massed in a terra cotta pot the sunflowers harmonize both in texture and color with the unglazed bowl. The shiny dark green camellia foliage and the flowers at different stages of growth inject variety into the design. The sunflowers with their interesting shapes are arranged on varying planes and in a three-dimensional manner to give volume.

Good Ikebana is good design. In the past overconcern with design led to the formulation of rigid arbitrary rules which restricted creativity and denied self-expression. Rules and principles should guide, not hinder and be ever-expanding in their application.

Fasciated hoop pine, cornflowers and leucadendron.

The radiator core from a wrecked automobile provided the container and the starting point for this arrangement. The fasciated hoop pine is in harmony with the twisted metal and the cornflowers and leucadendron flowers provide a color variation.

There are indeed those who copy the works of others and then act as though these are their own..... Influence and imitation are by no means the same thing. You may receive as much influence as you like—but you must digest it and make it your own. Non-digested influence is mere imitation..... Since no effort of your own is concerned this is the worst thing you can do. I would want everyone to understand that the sole way to creativity is the finding, through effort, of one's own self.

Hiroshi Teshigahara

Dodder vine and poinsettias.

The Dodder vine, a parasite with its massed lines and interesting color variations has been arranged to highlight the beautiful container made by Hiroshi Teshigahara, headmaster of the Sōgetsu School.

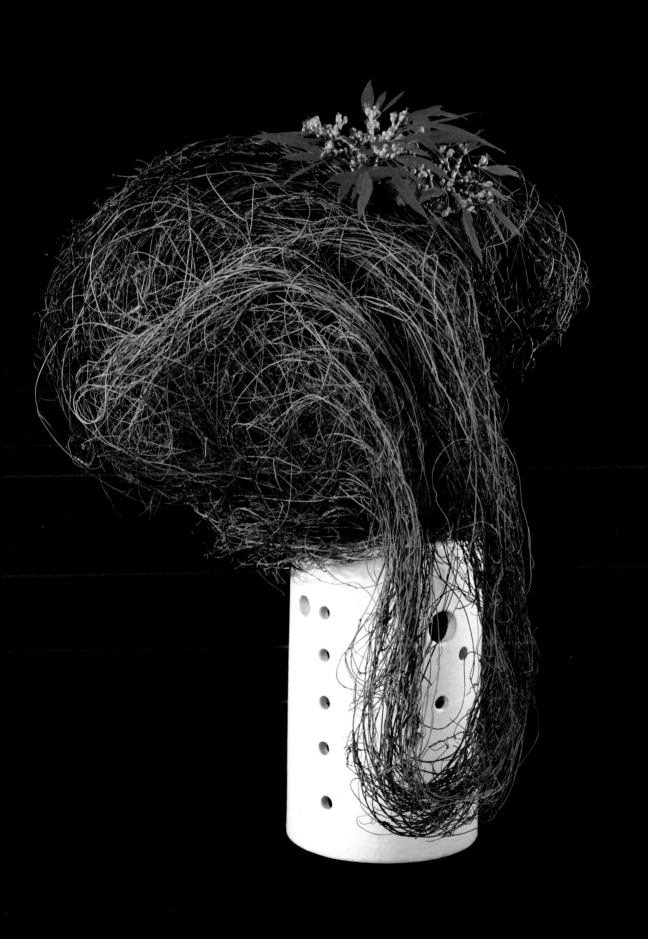

Ikebana is an awareness of nature resulting in an adventure with nature while trying to meet the challenge of nature.

Dodder vine and arum lilies.

The same Dodder vine used in the previous arrangement has been reorganized and arranged in harmony with the swirling lines of the Venini glass bowl. The two arum lilies appear to fly out of the arrangement.

It is possible when thinking of an arrangement to start from either the flowers or the vase. That is to say, if you have decided what flowers to use, an appropriate container for them will come to mind, and if you have already decided on a vase, you will also be able to choose suitable flowers. One thing is however, essential: the finished product should be one in which those particular flowers and that particular vase are indispensible.

Sofu

Strelitzia and lotus pods.

Two lotus pods are arranged to harmonize with the design of the container. Two strelitzias are used to provide color and a third dimension.

Ikebana is practiced for the inner spiritual satisfaction gained from the doing of it. The teacher opens the door. The student must find his own way. The way is "Kadō" the flower road and is a road without end. It is a beautiful but tantalizing road with many bends. Those who never get lost are rare indeed.

Albizzia pods and lasciandra.

Two lasciandra flowers and their leaves together with a stem of albizzia pods highlight the very modern container made by Yasuhara Kimey of Tokyo in 1950.

The maturation period in the study of Ikebana is slow and at times seemingly interminable. When the dawn of understanding breaks, the past is soon forgotten and it is as though the study has just begun.

Wisteria vine and hydrangea.

Mass and line are expressed in this arrangement of thick wisteria vine and hydrangeas in a large Indian pot.

In the study of Ikebana there are three styles known as *shin*, *gyō* and *sō*. These have sometimes been rendered as "formal", "semi-formal" and "informal" or straight, semi-cursive and cursive. As applied to Ikebana, the word *shin*, literally meaning "true", carries the idea of straightness or perpendicularity; the word *gyō* meaning "moving" connotes forceful linear movement. The same terms, deriving from calligraphy, are used with kindred values also in the seventeen syllable verse form the *haiku*, in painting and in Japanese garden art.

Pussy willow, pansies and violets.

A *Shin*-style arrangement of pansies, violets and pussy willow. The tall slender container was ideal for this style of arrangement. The pussy willow rises from the lower level to embrace the mass of pansies and violets.

Since Ikebana is closely connected with the seasons, it is of course possible to arrange the flowers as an expression of some seasonal aspect or other. There is, however, a common misconception that the seasons are the be all and end all of Ikebana. Nothing could be further from the truth. There are any number of other subjects which give ideal inspiration. Flowers, it is true, are inseparable from the seasons but this is not true of flower arrangement.

Sofu

Water lilies and sculpture.

An interesting root slightly changed in form by chiselling has been covered with copper shim and beaten. Providing an interesting piece of sculpture it has been arranged as though guarding the water lilies.

Man's aesthetic awareness is governed by his sensitivity to nature. In Ikebana we study basic principles inherent in nature in order to represent nature. In creative Ikebana we use nature as a medium to manifest our imagination ever mindful of the basic principles involved.

Dried sunflowers and dahlia.

Sunflowers, truly happy flowers, provide an excellent medium for Ikebana at all stages of their growth. Their diverse shapes, colors, sizes and textures comprise all of the ingredients to make an interesting arrangement whether used alone or combined with other material.

It is very difficult to be truly creative and at the same time to be a teacher. To be truly creative I believe one must devote all of one's time and energy to doing the "thing" to which one is dedicated. Yet if there were no teachers how could the art spread and flourish? Sofu was both a great artist and a great teacher.

Gypsophila and chrysanthemums.

Mass and line are expressed with two wire-mesh hemispheres, chrysanthemums and gypsophila. *Kasumi-sō* (mist-grass) the Japanese name for gypsophila aptly expresses the feeling of this lovely flower.

Your object in arranging flowers should be to create a lie, for in the context of Ikebana a lie becomes truth. By this I mean that a lie is just imagination, and Ikebana without imagination is worthless. Do not try to produce a facsimile of something in the material world, but rather give shape to those thoughts and feelings which exist within you. Flowers are concrete, but Ikebana is abstract.

Sofu

Scrap metal, daffodils and dried sunflowers.

Scrap metal dumps provide an interesting source both for accessory material and for making challenging containers. Here a rusted pick-head rests on some rusted wire complemented by a mass of yellow daffodils and dried sunflowers.

Shin, the name used for the primary branch by the Sōgetsu School is also used by the majority of Ikebana schools. It has its origin in classical Ikebana. Over the years it has been written in diverse ways but always with the reading of *shin*. Originally it was written with the character *kokoro* (心) meaning heart, connoting the core of man and hence the core of the arrangement. Later it was changed to *kami* (神) meaning God with the inference of reverence. During the 16th century it was changed to *makoto* (真) meaning sincerity, truth or straightness and has remained as such to the present day.

Poinciana pods and sunflowers.

The pods and container were chosen for their harmony of form. The two sunflowers accent the asymmetrical balance of the arrangement.

Ikebana is an awareness of nature. Some days in a familiar area you see things you have never noticed before and suddenly these previously unnoticed things become the inspiration for a new idea.

Pomegranates and scrap metal.

Two pieces of scrap metal have been combined to provide an interesting base for the two pomegranates and their leaves. The flat piece was chosen for its colorful rust markings and for its interesting mask-like appearance.

Principles never change but form is always changing. Basic principles provide a springboard for true creativity. It is relatively easy to teach basic principles. It is extremely difficult to teach creativity. In Ikebana the great masters teach by example hoping that the student will grasp the true spirit of the basic principles expressed in the example. In creative Ikebana the basic principles are not always apparent to the uninitiated nor to the student. This can only be achieved through a maturation of the creative experience.

Edgeworthia and strelitzia.

Wood sculpture made from the cut-ends of branches of Edgeworthia papyraferia known in Japanese as *mitsumata*. This is the same piece as used in the arrangement appearing on the jacket of the book. Here it has been re-arranged vertically and so given another dimension.

At heart I believe we all enjoy our romantic interludes. We envisage beautiful and dramatic masterpieces which in practice never quite seem to materialize. Theory should stimulate the urge to create for it is in the doing that the materials and the mood of the moment help formulate the design.

Scrap metal and sunflowers.

As mentioned previously, scrap metal dumps provide an ideal source for found objects. The rusty plough shear discs had been tied together with wire and discarded because of their bluntness. Their petal-like appearance provides a suitable base for the sunflowers. The discarded burnt-out section of a kerosene heater also provides a humorous yet complementary accessory for the sunflowers.

"*Ichirin*" or a one-flower arrangement is considered the quintessence of Ikebana. In classical Ikebana it is expressed in the arrangement of a single camellia and three and one-half leaves. It is also evocative of the austere simplicity of Zen as expressed in the tea ceremony. Mr. Sofu would on most occasions place an arrangement of a single flower or branch by the side of one of his massive sculptural masterpieces. I can remember on one occasion when preparing for an exhibition he said to me, "This large work has taken a great deal of time but this small arrangement of a single camellia was the more difficult."

Camellia.

A single camellia and its buds is arranged to harmonize with
the container.

A lack of originality is fatal. Instead of copying what has already been created, one should try to make the best of one's natural talent and individuality. This is not easy to do but without trying one will never find one's way toward creativity..... There is no easy way and nothing is to be attained through imitation.

Hiroshi Teshigahara

Dried aspidistra leaves and poppies.

Probably the most durable of all leaves, the aspidistra provides infinite possibilities for its arrangement. Arranged here in a wave-like fashion they have been complemented with a small mass of poppies.

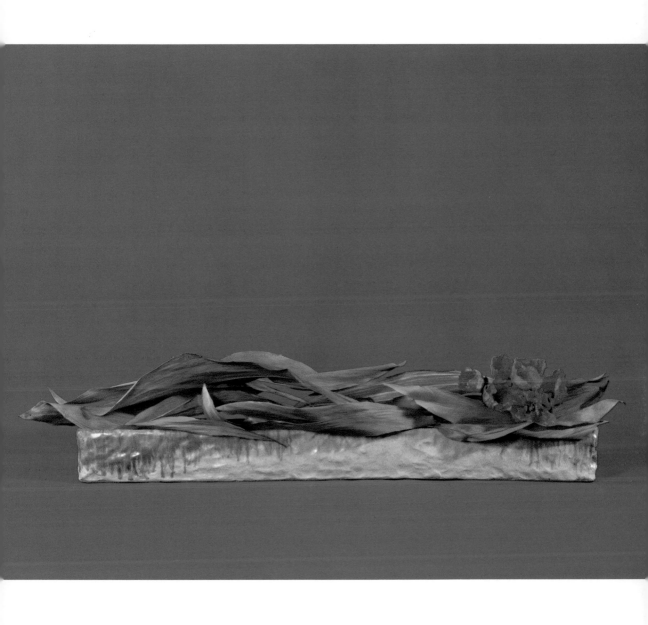

Try using leaves in your arrangement. Flowers may delude you as to their real character, but you can rely on the leaves to express the true essence of the plant.

Sofu

Dried aspidistra leaves and poppies.

Arranged in a similar fashion to the previous arrangement, a variation has been given by threading the poppies through the leaves in an upright fashion to display their interesting lines.

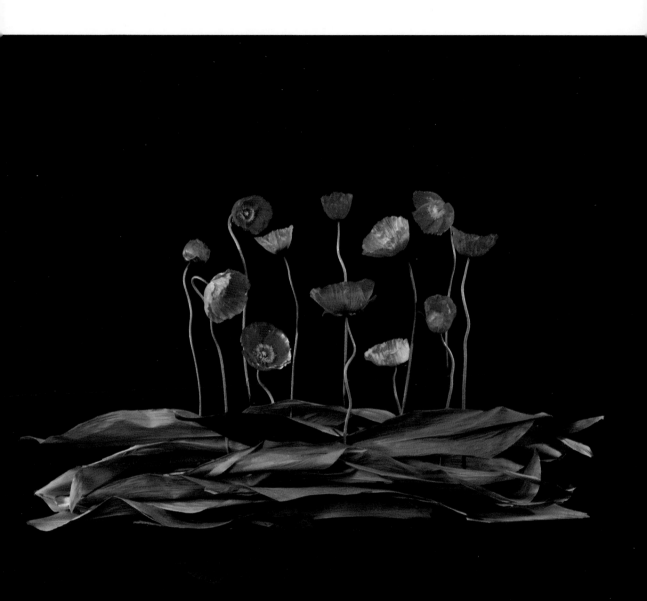

Variety in unity is a basic principle of all art. This principle is beautifully expressed in nature. A rose is beautiful because of three elements—line, surface and mass (color being an integral part of the mass). The stem provides line, the leaves surface, and the flower mass. The total of these three elements equals perfection. The elimination of any one element destroys the unified whole.

Roses, asparagus fern and edgeworthia.

Edgeworthia (*mitsumata*) asparagus fern and Sonia roses have been knitted together at the mouth of the container to form this *nageire* (vase) style arrangement.

There have been many forms of Ikebana in the past and there will probably be many more in the future. This process of development is inevitable as long as Ikebana remains closely associated with our daily life. The essential spirit of Ikebana will, I hope, continue forever, but I do not think the preservation of any one form to be of prime importance.

Sofu

Scrap metal and cornflowers.

Introduced into class by a student, radiator cores from wrecked automobiles add another dimension to found objects. Combined into a sculptural form on a metal base they have been highlighted with a small mass of cornflowers.

Shin, *soe* and *hikae* are the names used for the three primary branches of a Sōgetsu arrangement. The placement of the *shin* branch decides the character of the arrangement. *Soe* from the verb *soeru*, to support, is arranged to give depth to the arrangement. The correct placement of the *hikae*, derived from the verb *hikaeru* to modify, gives the arrangement its quality.

Palm spathes and acacia.

Palm spathes have been placed in a sculptural form in a large flat brown container and laced with acacia. The clipped palm spathe extending upward is a good example of the *shin* line. The *soe* projects forward and down the front of the container. The *hikae* extends to the left below the *shin*.

Ikebana is a meaningful activity. It makes definite statements about man's feeling for nature. The trained Ikebana artist should be able to turn his hand to any kind of material which can be used to create good design.

Scrap metal and sunflower.

Scrap metal is infinite in its usage. Here a piece of rusty chain forms an excellent support for the sunflower. The metal bar adds dimension to the assemblage.

We all learn from each other providing a circle of knowledge. Students learn from teachers, teachers from masters, masters from grand masters and grand masters from masters, teachers and students and so the circle is complete. The greatest reward for a teacher is to see a student successful.

Stirrups, bit and woody pear.

Stirrups, a bit and five woody pears are combined to make an interesting sculpture.

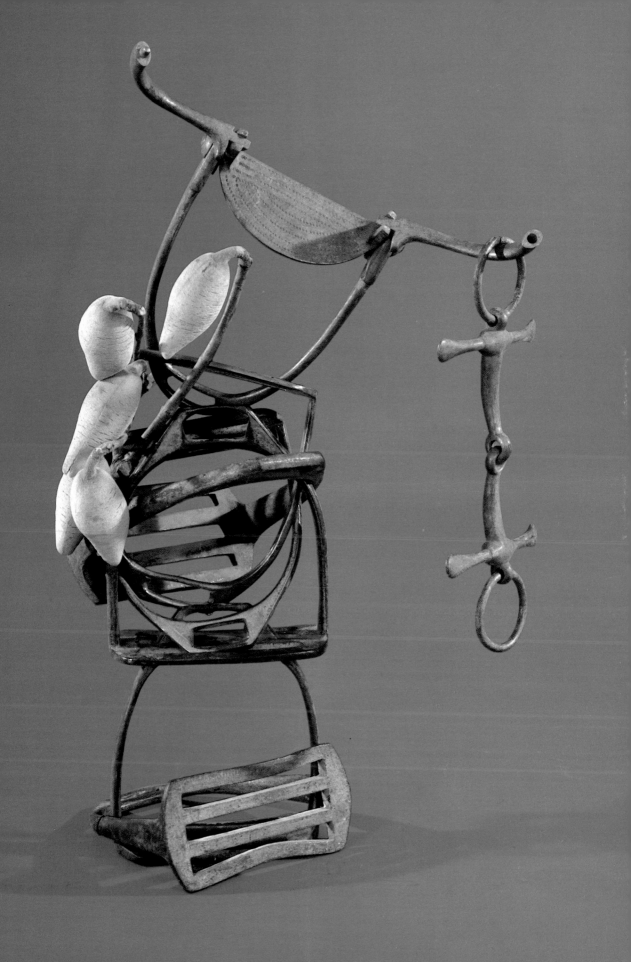

To the average person a flower is no more than a passive element of nature whose sole function is to be admired. To think that, however, is to miss the vital fact that flowers have something to convey to the viewer and must, therefore, be not only admired, but understood. Since every flower has its own character and mood it can convey subtle hints of myriad realms beyond the everyday world.

Sofu

Camellias.

The camellia, probably the most beautiful of flowers is among the most difficult to arrange. In this arrangement the handles of the basket are an important part of the design.

During the preparation of this book I was privileged to meet Marcel Marceau, the great French mime, who visited my studio through the courtesy of one of my students. I sincerely believe him to be one of the two most sensitively artistic men I have met. He immediately showed great empathy for Ikebana and I felt I had known him for years. He said, "I am often asked if I ever tire of repeatedly performing one of my acts, "Creation", and I reply—never. Each time I perform, for me it is my first performance. The movement of my hands is never the same." This is also true of Ikebana. The genus of flower may be the same but the arrangement is always different.

Japonica and camellias.

Japonica and camellias are a popular Japanese combination in Ikebana. The beautiful lines and small flowers of the Japonica harmonize with the larger camellia flowers in the interesting terra-cotta container.

One of the differences I have noticed between the Japanese student and the Western student is that the Japanese is content to watch and learn by repetition. The Westerner, with a seemingly more inquisitive mind, learns by logic and wants to know Why? and asks many questions. On one occasion I asked my classical master why the school used only a maximum of fifteen aspidistra leaves and not seventeen or even more. He replied: "Around the fifteenth of the month the moon is full and that is perfection but if you feel you can arrange more perfectly, please do." After thirty years of study I am still endeavoring to master the fifteen leaves.

Dried aspidistra leaves, acacia and Dutch iris.

Designed to express color harmony, the dried aspidistra leaves have been combined with Dutch iris and acacia. The acacia, popularly known in Australia as Wattle is Australia's national flower.

It is a common, although not quite correct, belief that in Ikebana the Japanese invariably use an odd number of flowers or branches and particularly avoid using four pieces of material. These beliefs are probably based on the Principle of Three as expressed in *Ten* (heaven), *Chi* (earth) and *Jin* (man) with its cosmic connotations of the harmony of the universe and of the fact that *shi*, the word for four, can also mean death. It is true that in modern Ikebana the basic form is based on a scalene triangle comprised of three branches of unequal lengths but any number of supporting branches may be added. And as for "four", the Japanese ideographs for "four" and for "death" are quite different. A true understanding of this misconception may best be comprehended through the words of the great master Sofu: "Harmony and balance are far more important than odd or even numbers."

Nandina and Iris:

The lace-like foliage of the nandina is in harmony with the basket and is complemented by the bud and flower of the beautiful Japanese iris.

There is an erroneous belief held by many people that all Ikebana arrangements have some hidden meaning. This is not so. Ikebana is practiced for the inner spiritual satisfaction gained from the doing of it. Flowers and trees in their natural environment are beautiful indeed however when we compress these branches and flowers into a natural scene in a vase we give them order and harmony.

Sunflowers.

Two sunflowers arranged in the double-shin style in a modern container. The shape of the container is in harmony with and emphasizes the sunflowers.

The beauty and dignity which one can see in a face lined with age and a body bent with years of hard work are also present in a withered flower and it is for this reason that such a bloom may be used in Ikebana. However, just as a face which is blackened and coarsened with dissipation is ugly, so is a flower which is beginning to droop, since it calls to mind a picture of gradual decay.

Sofu

Fox-face (Solanum mammosum) *and dried monstera and strelitzia.*

This humorous udder-like plant popular for its interest and brilliant color is arranged with dried monstera leaves and two strelitzias. The fox-face was the motivating idea for the design. The other materials and the container were chosen to accent the color and form of the fox-face.

CHAN Yen-yuan, historian of art in the ninth century wrote "Now the *yin* and *yang* fashion and form all things..." *In*—shade and *yō*—sun are the Japanese readings of the same two characters and form an integral part of Ikebana. In the dualistic pre-classical philosophy of China as expounded in the *I-ching* or "Book of Changes", *in* (*yin*) is the negative, passive or female principle; *yō* (*yang*), the positive, active or male principle. The phenomenal world is viewed as pervaded by these two contrary yet complementary forces; negative and positive are attributes of all things, some things being negative while others are positive. Ideally there is a perfect balance between the two, for order reigns in the cosmos as long as the positive is in proportion with the negative, disorder accompanying the predominance of one over the other. In Ikebana the ideal is to endeavor to create one harmonious whole through the manipulation of these two forces.

Albizzia pods, verticordia and monstera.

This single branch of Albizzia pods expresses the interesting patterns found in natural forms. The orange verticordia is in color harmony with the pods and container. The monstera leaf provides both a textural and color contrast.

There is a common tendency among Western students to relate all flower arrangements to their homes. The home should be subordinated to the study, not the goal. Ikebana never has been a mere decoration. Inspired by *Shumisen* the mythical Mount Mehru of the Buddhist and Hindu cosmology, Rikka from its inception in the mid-fifteenth century was designed to express the glory and majesty of Nature. Initially practiced by the Japanese nobility, Buddhist priests and the warrior class, over the ensuing years Ikebana has had a coherent development moving with the times as a living art should. It has developed along lines so diversified that no facet of Japanese life remains untouched by its presence.

Eucalyptus bark and strelitzia.

A rusted metal ring has been used to combine three pieces of bark and four strelitzias in a sculptural form.

Found objects may be aptly termed "Nature's sculpture". Expressions of their environment they show the effect of the wind, the sun, the sea, fire and disease. These elements work against perfect symmetry and so the principles of *yin* and *yang* control the balance of Nature's asymmetry.

Root and hoop pine.

Nature's sculpture is an apt term for many found objects. This Mallee root was grubbed from the ground and cleaned. Mounted on two plough-shear discs and crowned with some hoop pine it provides a provocative image to stimulate the imagination.

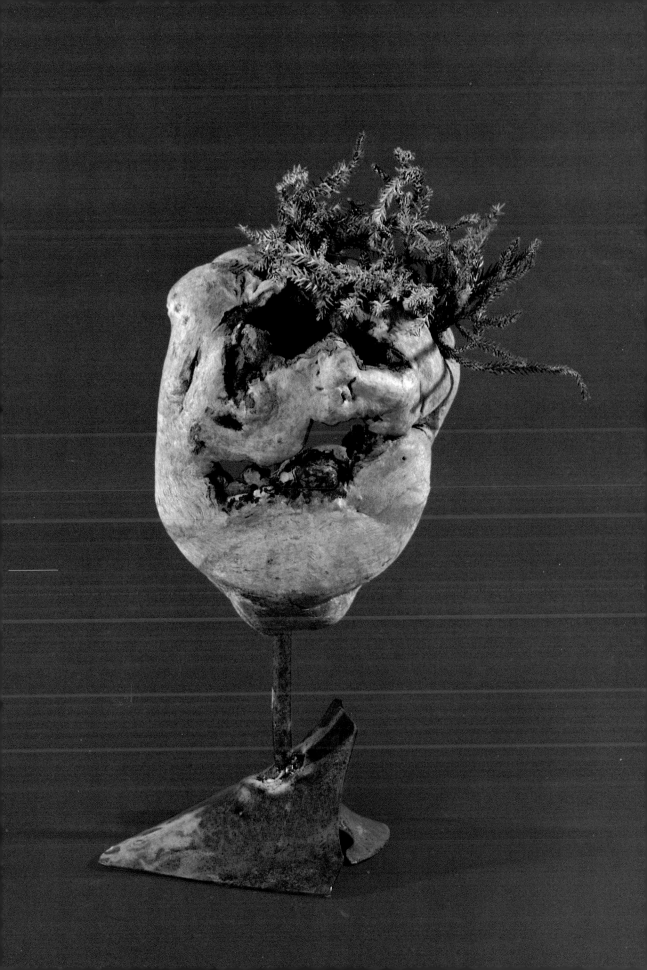

The word *ikeru* as applied to Ikebana has the implication of change or the creation of shape. Thus the central problem of Ikebana is how to change the material which one is using and how to create a new shape from this change. When you can appreciate the fact that beautiful flowers, plus an attractive vase, do not necessarily equal good Ikebana you will then understand the object of studying the art of flower arrangement.

Sofu

Aspidistra leaves, daisies and cornflowers.

Four aspidistra leaves have been tied with part of a leaf, shredded and placed across the bowl over the daisies and cornflowers.

The three geometric symbols the circle, the square and the triangle are used by the Sōgetsu School to identify the three primary branches. The *shin* (○) the *soe* (□) and the *hikae* (△). In classical Ikebana the circle denotes tree material, the square, flowers and the triangle, large leaves. Their spiritual symbolism is expressed in heaven, the triangle; man, the circle and earth, the square or more correctly, the rectangle. With the addition of a half-circle (water) and a lotus-bud shape (fire) they symbolize the five elements of the universe as expressed in ancient Japanese cosmology —sky, wind, fire, water and earth. It is from this that the five storied pagoda and the Japanese lantern developed.

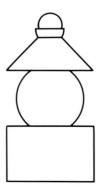

Monstera leaf and agiratum.

The ceramic sculpture provides the focal point of this design. The monstera leaf is arranged in a plume-like fashion with the agiratum providing color.

I have said that every flower has its own mood but it would, perhaps, be truer to say that it has an infinite number of possible moods since what it suggests is really a matter for individual interpretation. The basic fact is, however, that the person who is able to receive some form of evocative stimulus when looking at flowers will find that he has discovered the means of escaping into a dream world of his own creation. Those who practice the art of flower arrangement very often attain such a state, for, in the course of their art they obtain constant inspiration from the flowers.

Sofu

Carnations and metal strapping.

Metal strapping from a carton has been attached in a free-form manner to repeat the design on this modern container made by Suzuki Osamu of Kyoto in 1950. Five white carnations have been massed behind the strapping to complete the black and white motif of the design.

The Sōgetsu School has always required its teachers to demonstrate from behind the arrangement. This is not only better for the audience but it insures that the teacher if he is to be successful, must master the basic principles and therefore be endowed with a springboard for true creativeness.

Iris Orientalis (formerly Ochroleuca)

Two flowers and two leaves of the Iris Orientalis have been subordinated to the challenging six-part container. The five tubes can be moved along the metal rod according to the designer's mood. The two leaves have been arranged in a horizontal manner in harmony with the container. The flowers provide color and accent.

The fact that Ikebana was conceived in Japan is probably attributable to various favorable conditions that were prevalent in this country. One cannot, however say that Ikebana belongs only to Japan. On the contrary its world is boundless.

Sofu

Pussy willow and camellia.

The container suggested the idea for this design. The camellia (*mihata* "Red Flag") is in harmony with the center hole and the pussy willow has been curved to harmonize with the shape of the container.

PART TWO : BASIC LESSONS

The lessons presented here in pictorial form should be carefully studied and their basic principles mastered. Not only will such mastery enable the student to have knowledge of a number of beautiful arrangements but this knowledge will lead the arranger to develop his own creative ability—for the lessons are but the foundation on which the greater structure of creativity and free expression rests.

The lessons are based on two fundamental styles, *moribana* and *nageire*. *Moribana* is a compound formation from the verb *moru* "to heap up" and the noun *hana* "flower(s)", and hence means "heaped-up flowers." This style of arrangement features a low, shallow container in which the material is held in place by a needle-point holder termed *kenzan*. *Nageire* is derived from the verb *nage-ireru*, meaning "to throw (fling) into". It features a tall container in which the material rests against the lip of the container or is held in place by various artifices which will be dealt with as the occasion arises. In this style of arrangement a needle-point holder is not used.

In both the *moribana* and *nageire* styles, the arrangement is based on the asymmetrical placement of three principal branches—the *shin* (primary branch), the *soe* (secondary branch), and the *hikae* (tertiary branch). All supporting branches are termed *jūshi*. The lengths of these three branches are determined by the type of plant material, the container and the location of the completed arrangement. The *shin* may be from one to two times the container's length plus its height. For tall containers the *shin* may be from one to two times the container's height plus its diameter. In an average arrangement the *shin* is one and one-half times the container's length or height plus the container's height or diameter. The *soe* is three-quarters the length of the *shin* and the *hikae* is three-quarters the length of the *soe*. In large arrangements the *hikae* may be half the length of the *soe*.

While these measurements are sound proportions for any student to follow they are only approximate. When the lessons have been mastered the arranger may at times rely on his own judgment.

There are no restrictions in the use or combination of plant life. This is governed by color harmony, texture and good taste. However, the beginner would be wise to show restraint and limit himself either to one or two kinds of flowers or to a combination of one kind of foliage and one kind of flower. Although there are no restrictions, combinations of more than three varieties of material are rarely used. Non-flowering material such as the pine or willow is seldom used alone. However tree material which bears blossoms, such as the Japanese quince, is often used alone.

When two kinds of material are used it is common practice for the tertiary branch (*hikae*) to be of different material from the primary and secondary branches (*shin* and *soe*).

The following are important basic features of good modern arrangements:
1. The needle-point holder should not be visible.
2. Study your material carefully and select the best branch or flower for the *shin*. The *shin* will decide the style of the arrangement and whether it is to be a left-hand or a right-hand arrangement.
3. Trim your branches or flowers carefully but do not destroy the natural character of the material.
4. Give the arrangement strength at the base to give it a feeling of growth.
5. Be guided by the angles of placement when arranging the material in order that the arrangement is three-dimensional.
6. Endeavor to commune with the material and so endow the arrangement with feeling.
7. For naturalistic arrangements lightly cover the lip of the container with foliage or flowers.
8. Arrange your material as though it is growing to the sun.
9. As a general rule when using non-flowering branch material for the *shin* and *soe* use a flower for the *hikae*. This injects variety into the triangle.
10. Remember *moribana* grows; *nageire* flows.

Fig. 1

Fig. 2

Fig. 3

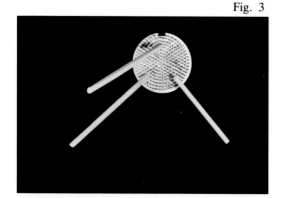

LESSON 1.   MORIBANA.   BASIC UPRIGHT
STYLE.

*Material: nut grass and
chrysanthemums.*

Fig. 1.   The shin or primary branch is
approximately twice the width plus the
height of the container. The *soe* or secondary branch is three-quarters the length of
the *shin*. The *hikae* or tertiary branch is
three-quarters the length of *soe*. The remaining two flowers and branches are
termed *jūshi*. While there are no set rules
for the length or number of *jūshi*, they
should not be longer than any one of the
three main branches which they support. In
this lesson the flowers support the *hikae*
which is the shortest of the three main
branches and the branches support the *soe*.

Fig. 2.   The positions of the three main
branches. The needle-point holder is placed
in the left front of the container. The *shin* is
placed at an angle of 15° toward the left
shoulder. The *soe* is placed at an angle of 45°
toward the left shoulder, just a little to the
left front of the *shin*. The *hikae* is placed at
an angle of 75° toward the right shoulder
just a little to the right front of the *shin*.

To complete the arrangement, add the
supporting material with a forward movement. The needle-point holder should not
be visible.

Fig. 3.   A bird's eye view of the positions
of the three main branches.

Fig. 1

Fig. 2

Fig. 3

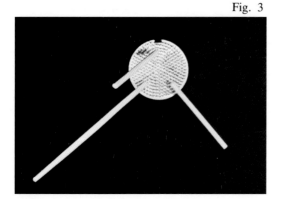

LESSON 2.   MORIBANA.   BASIC SLANTING STYLE.

Material: five roses.

Fig. 1.   As the container is large, the *shin* or primary stem is approximately the length plus the height of the container. The *soe* or secondary stem is three-quarters the length of the *shin*. The *hikae* or tertiary stem is three-quarters the length of the *soe*. The two other roses constitute the *jūshi* or supporting flowers.

Fig. 2.   The positions of the three main branches. The needle-point holder is placed to the right rear of the container. The *shin* is placed at an angle of 45° toward the left shoulder.
The *soe* is placed at an angle of 15° toward the left shoulder.
The *hikae* is placed at an angle of 75° toward the right shoulder.

The arrangement is completed by adding the remaining two roses. The needle-point holder should not be visible.
This form differs from the Upright Style of Lesson 1 in that the positions of the *shin* and *soe* have been reversed.

Fig. 3.   A bird's-eye view of the positions of the three main branches.

104 Basic Lessons

Fig. 1

Fig. 2

Fig. 3

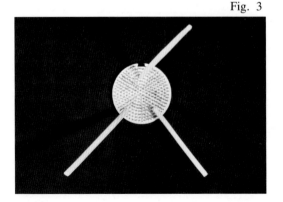

LESSON 3. MORIBANA. UPRIGHT STYLE, FIRST VARIATION.

Material: umbrella grass and anthuriums.

Fig. 1. The long branch of umbrella grass is the *shin*, its length being approximately twice the length plus the height of the container. The *soe* is three-quarters the length of the *shin* while the *hikae* is three-quarters the length of the *soe*. The remaining four stems comprise the *jūshi* or supporting material.

Fig. 2. The positions of the three main branches. The *shin* is placed at an angle of 15° to the right rear. The *soe* is placed at an angle of 45° toward the left shoulder. The *hikae* is placed at an angle of 75° toward the right shoulder.

The arrangement is completed by placing the remaining stems of grass and the anthuriums at the base of the arrangement and in support of the *shin*. Again, the needle-point holder should not be visible.

Fig. 3. A bird's-eye view of the positions of the three main branches.

Fig. 1

Fig. 2

Fig. 3

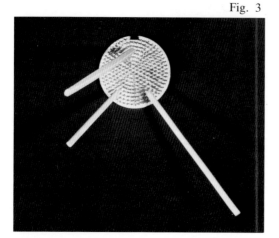

LESSON 4.   MORIBANA.   UPRIGHT STYLE,
SECOND
VARIATION.

*Material: nandina and
dahlias.*

Fig. 1.   The length of the *shin* or primary branch is approximately one and one-half times the length plus the height of the container. The *soe* or secondary branch is three-quarters the length of the *shin*, the *hikae* or tertiary branch is three-quarters the length of the *soe*. The remaining nandina and dahlias comprise the *jūshi* or supporting material.

Fig. 2.   The positions of the three main branches. The *shin* is placed at an angle of 15° toward the left shoulder. The *soe* is placed at an angle of 75° toward the right shoulder. The *hikae* is placed at an angle of 45° toward the left shoulder.

The arrangement is completed by adding the remaining dahlias and nandina at the base of the arrangement and in support of the *shin*, *soe* and *hikae*.

Fig. 3.   A bird's-eye view of the positions of the three main branches.

Fig. 1

Fig. 2

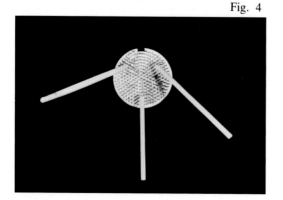

Fig. 3

Fig. 4

LESSON 5.   MORIBANA.   UPRIGHT STYLE, THIRD VARIATION.

Material: three roses.

Fig. 1.   The length of the *shin* stem is the length plus the height of the container. The *soe* stem is three-quarters the length of the *shin*, the *hikae* stem, three-quarters the length of the *soe*. As the container is made of glass, the needle-point holder is wrapped in white tissue paper; this aids considerably in concealing the holder from view.

Fig. 2.   The *shin* inclines at an angle of 15° toward the left shoulder.

Fig. 3.   The *soe* inclines at an angle of 45° toward the right shoulder. The *hikae* inclines at an angle of 75° directly toward the viewer. A few leaves should cover the edge of the container and care should be exercised to eliminate unnecessary leaves. Too many leaves or leaves that are too large will spoil the arrangement.

Fig. 4.   A bird's-eye view of the positions of the three main branches.

Fig. 1

Fig. 2

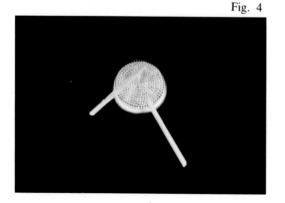

Fig. 3

Fig. 4

LESSON 6.   MORIBANA.   UPRIGHT STYLE,
FOURTH
VARIATION.

Material: Iris Orientalis.

Fig. 1.   This form of arrangement consists of only two of the usual three branches: a *shin* and a *hikae*. No *soe* is used. In this arrangement, two supporting leaves have been used with the *shin*. The length of the *shin* is twice the length plus the height of the container. The length of the iris *hikae* remains in the same ratio as though a *soe* were used.

Fig. 2.   The *shin* is placed at an angle of 15° toward the left shoulder.

Fig. 3.   The arrangement is completed by placing the *hikae* at an angle of 75° toward the right shoulder and by placing the remaining flower and leaves at the base of the arrangement.

Fig. 4.   A bird's-eye view of the positions of the two main branches.

Fig. 1

Fig. 2

Fig. 3

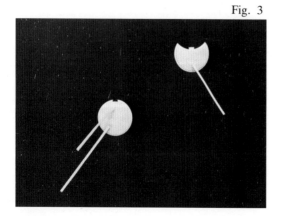

LESSON 7.　MORIBANA.　UPRIGHT STYLE, FIFTH VARIATION.

Material:　tea-tree and tiger lilies.

Fig. 1.　This style of arrangement is done in two parts. The *shin* and the *soe* are placed in one holder, the *hikae* in another. The *shin* is approximately the length plus the height of the container. The *soe* is three-quarters the length of the *shin*. The lilies comprise the *hikae*, the longest of which is three-quarters the length of the *soe*.

Fig. 2.　The positions of the three main branches. One needle-point holder is placed to the left front of the container, the other to the right rear. The *shin* is placed in the left holder and inclines at an angle of 15° toward the left shoulder. The *soe* is placed to the left front of the *shin* and at an angle of 45° toward the left shoulder. The *hikae* lily is placed at an angle of 75° toward the right shoulder.

The arrangement is completed by placing the remaining material in support of the *shin*, *soe* and *hikae*.

Fig. 3.　A bird's-eye view of the positions of the three main branches.

Fig. 1

Fig. 2

Fig. 3

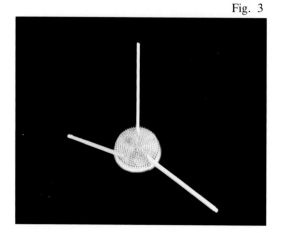

LESSON 8.   MORIBANA.   UPRIGHT STYLE,
SIXTH
VARIATION.

*Material: gypsophila and
roses.*

Fig. 1.   This style of arrangement is viewable from all angles. The *shin* is approximately the width plus the depth of the basket. The *soe* is three-quarters the length of the *shin* and the *hikae* is three-quarters the length of the *soe*. The remaining roses and gypsophila are used as support material or *jūshi*.

Fig. 2.   The positions of the three main branches. The *shin* is placed at an angle of 15° toward the left shoulder. The *soe* is placed at an angle of 45° to the right shoulder. The *hikae* is placed at an angle of 75° toward the center rear.

To complete the arrangement the remaining material is placed forward and back in support of the three main branches in order that the arrangement may be viewed from any angle without the needle-point holder being visible.

Fig. 3.   A bird's-eye view of the positions of the three main branches.

116 Basic Lessons

Fig. 1

Fig. 2

Fig. 3

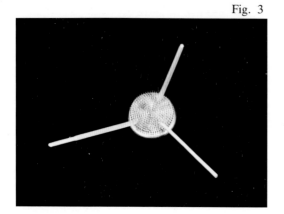

Material: carnations and umbrella fern.

Fig. 1.   The *shin* carnation is approximately the length plus the height of the container. The *soe* is three-quarters the length of the *shin* and the *hikae* is three-quarters the length of the *soe*.

Fig. 2.   The positions of the three main branches. The *shin* is inclined at 45° to the left front. The *soe* is inclined at 15° to the right rear. The *hikae* is inclined at 75° to the right front.

The arrangement is completed by adding the *jūshi* of carnations and umbrella fern. The needle-point holder should not be visible.

Fig. 3.   A bird's-eye view of the three main branches.

Fig. 1

Fig. 2

Fig. 3

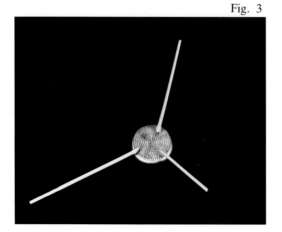

LESSON 10.   MORIBANA.   HORIZONTAL
STYLE,
SIXTH VARIATION.

Material: Lilium
longiflorum.

Fig. 1.   The *shin* is approximately the length plus the depth of the container. The *soe* is three-quarters the length of the *shin* and the *hikae* is three-quarters the length of the *soe*. The remaining lilies comprise the supporting material.

Fig. 2.   The positions of the three main stems. The *shin* inclines at an angle of 85° to the left front. The *soe* inclines at an angle of 65° to the right rear and the *hikae* inclines at an angle of 75° toward the right front.

To complete the arrangement the remaining lilies are placed forward and back in support of the three main branches in order that the arrangement may be viewed from any angle without the needle-point holder being visible.

Fig. 3.   A bird's-eye view of the positions of the three main branches.

LESSON 11.   FLOATING ARRANGEMENT.

*Material: carnations and
miscanthus.*

This arrangement is distinguished by its plant material floating in water. The material may be placed either in mass or may float freely, to one side or at the center of the container as desired. Almost any kind of floral material, either leaves or flowers, can be used effectively in this manner. In this particular arrangement miscanthus grass and three carnations have been used. A floating arrangement is known as *uki-bana*.

Another style of arrangement included in this category but not illustrated here, is the "spreading" arrangement (*shiki-bana*) in which flowers and leaves are arranged directly on a table without a container, needle-point holder, or water. This form is suitable as a table arrangement for a short while only.

LESSON 12.   MORIMONO.

Material: ribbon grass,
eggplant, pepper,
apple, orange and
Singapore orchid.

Morimono is an arrangement of fruit,
fruit and flowers, fruit and vegetables,
vegetables or vegetables and flowers. The
arrangement shown here has been made on
two straw mats. The arrangement may be
made in or on almost any kind of container
be it bowl, basket, mat, straw, lid or large
natural leaf, such as banana or monstera.

Morimono differs from a "spreading
arrangement" in that its choice of materials
is not restricted to flowers and that it is
usually on a base of some sort.

Morimono, Floating and Spreading
arrangements all should be arranged in the
basic pattern of the asymmetrical triangle.

Fig. 1

Fig. 2

Fig. 3

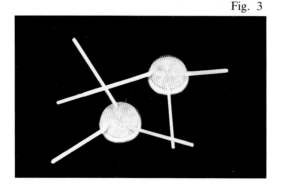

LESSON 13.   MORIBANA.   EIGHTH
VARIATION,
TWO-CONTAINER
ARRANGEMENT.

*Material: gypsophila and
roses.*

This effective and versatile style is made by combining any two basic styles, in this instance the third variation slanting and the first variation slanting. Another striking arrangement is obtained by combining a tall vase with a low *moribana* style. From the basic styles many beautiful combinations can be developed.

Fig. 1.   Gypsophila is used for the right arrangement while roses are used for the left arrangement. The length of the *shin* of the gypsophila of the larger arrangement is governed by the placement of the two containers. The relative lengths of the three primary branches of the two arrangements can be gauged from the photograph. The *soe* is three-quarters the length of the *shin* and the *hikae* is three-quarters the length of the *soe*. The gypsophila and two roses on the right are the supporting material or *jūshi*.

Fig. 2.   The positions of the three main branches in each container. In the right container the *shin* stem of gypsophila is placed at 45° toward the left shoulder. The *soe* inclines at 15° toward the right shoulder. The *hikae* inclines at 75° directly to the front. In the left container the *shin* rose inclines at 45° toward the right shoulder. The *soe* inclines at 15° to the left rear. The *hikae* inclines at 75° toward the left shoulder.

The arrangement is completed by placing the supporting gypsophila in the right arrangement and the remaining two roses in the left arrangement.

Fig. 3.   A bird's-eye view of the positions of the three main branches in each needle-point holder.

Fig. 1

Fig. 2

Fig. 3

Fig. 4

LESSON 14.   NAGEIRE.   BASIC UPRIGHT
STYLE

Material: spirea and roses.

Nageire, which is one of the oldest forms of Japanese flower arrangement, differs from *moribana* in two important points. First, a tall container is used instead of the low flat container used in *moribana*; secondly, no needle-point holder is used. However, the same basic principles of *moribana* apply, that is, three principal branches are used and foliage is used at the mouth or lip of the container.

Fig. 1.   The length of the *shin*, primary branch, is approximately twice the height plus the width of the container. In order to hold the branch in position an extension approximately the height of the vase, is attached to the *shin* branch. This is done by splitting the ends of the two branches and inserting one branch into the other as illustrated.

Fig. 2.   The *shin* together with the extension but without the needle-point holder, is placed in the vase and inclines at an angle of 15° toward the left shoulder.

Fig. 3.   The *soe* is three-quarters the length of the shin and inclines at 45° toward the left shoulder.

Fig. 4.   The *hikae* is three-quarters the length of the *soe* and inclines at 75° toward the right shoulder.

The arrangement is completed by adding the two supporting roses and a branch of spirea in support of the *shin*.

Fig. 1

Fig. 2

Fig. 3

Fig. 4

Fig. 5

LESSON 15.   NAGEIRE.   BASIC SLANTING
STYLE.

*Material: privet and Lilium
longiflorum.*

Fig. 1.   The length of the *shin* of privet is approximately one and one-half times the height plus the width of the vase. That of the *soe*, three-quarters the length of the *shin*, and that of the *hikae* lily three-quarters the length of the *soe*. The two lilies used for *jūshi* (supporting branches) are shorter than the *hikae* lilies.

Fig. 2.   Two twigs are placed criss-cross in the mouth of the container forming four quadrants. This enables the branches to stay in place without falling down into the container.

Fig. 3.   The *shin* is placed at an angle of 45° toward the left shoulder. It is placed in the top left quadrant with the stem resting against the wall of the container.

Fig. 4.   The *soe* is placed in the same quadrant but at an angle of 15° toward the left shoulder.

Fig. 5.   The *hikae* is placed at an angle of 75° toward the right shoulder.

The arrangement is completed by placing the stem of two lilies with a forward movement at the mouth of the container one to the rear of the other to give depth.

INDEX

Acacia, 19, 21, 65, 75
Agiratum, 91
Albizzia pod, 33, 83
Anthurium, 107
Apple, 125
Arum lily, 29
Asparagus fern, 61
Aspidistra leaves, 57, 59, 75, 89

Banksia, 19

Camellia, 23, 55, 71, 73, 97
Carnation, 93, 119, 123
Chrysanthemum, 43, 103
Cornflower, 25, 63, 89

Daffodil, 45
Dahlia, 41, 109
Daisy, 89
Dried aspidistra leaves, 57, 59, 75
Dried monstera, 81
Dried sunflower, 41, 45
Dodder vine, 27, 29
Dutch iris, 75

Edgeworthia, 51, 61
Eggplant, 125
Eucalyptus, 19, 21
Eucalyptus bark, 85

Fasciated hoop pine, 25
Fox-face, 81

Gypsophila, 43, 117, 127

Hoop pine, 87
Hydrangea, 35

Iris, 77
Iris Orientalis, 113

Japonica, 73

Lasciandra, 33
Leucadendron, 25
Lilium longiflorum, 131
Lotus pod, 31

Metal strapping, 93
Miscanthus, 123
Monstera, 81, 83, 91

Nandina, 77, 109
Nut grass, 103

Orange, 125

Palm spathes, 65
Pansy, 37
Pepper, 125
Pine, 25
Poinciana, 47
Poinsettia, 21, 27
Pomegranate, 49
Poppy, 57, 59
Privet, 131
Pussy willow, 37, 97

Ribbon grass, 125
Root, 87
Rose, 61, 105, 111, 117, 127, 129

Scrap metal, 45, 49, 53, 63, 67
Sculpture, 39
Sculptured root, 19
Singapore orchid, 125
Spirea, 129
Stirrup, 69
Strelitzia, 31, 51, 81, 85
Sunflower, 23, 41, 47, 67, 79

Tea-tree, 115
Tiger lily, 115

Umbrella grass, 107
Umbrella fern, 119

Verticordia, 83
Violet, 37

Water lily, 39
Weeping mulberry, 21
Wisteria vine, 35
Woody pear, 69